Trace of One

Trace

Poems by JOANNA GOODMAN

# of One

UNIVERSITY OF IOWA PRESS  *Iowa City*

University of Iowa Press, Iowa City 52242

Copyright © 2002 by Joanna Goodman

Printed in the United States of America

Design by Richard Hendel

http://www.uiowa.edu/~uipress

The publication of this book was generously
supported by the University of Iowa Foundation.

Printed on acid-free paper

Library of Congress
Cataloging-in-Publication Data
Goodman, Joanna, 1968–
Trace of one: poems / by Joanna Goodman.
p.   cm. — (Iowa poetry prize)
ISBN 0-87745-806-5 (pbk.)
I. Title.   II. Series.
PS3607.O57 T73   2002
811'.6 — dc21   2001054279

02 03 04 05 06 P 5 4 3 2 1

For Lailah, who makes it all sweet again

just look

so much un-windowed

over there . . .

    Paul Celan,

    The Darkened

CONTENTS

II

ACKNOWLEDGMENTS

Grateful acknowledgment is made to the editors of the following journals in which some of these poems first, or will soon, appear:

Nation: "Tebaide"; "In an Excessive Corridor"
Tin House: "Coming of Age"
Literary Review: "The Succession of Parts"; "Coming Up Violets";
  "Pian dell'Arca"; "This Is Joy"; "Take Aim"; "Examples of Use";
  "Resuscitation"; "Benares"; "Home"; "Trace of One"; "Beech Tree
  in March"; "Falser Certainty"
Fence: "The Aftermath"; "Departure"
Phoebe: "Wave"
Sonora Review: "Watermark"
Indiana Review: "What Brought Them There"
Massachusetts Review: "The Dry Spell"

My deep gratitude to my parents, my sister, my friends and teachers who have guided and supported me during the writing of these poems. Particular thanks to Tucker Malarkey for listening and advising with her heart and to Henry Israeli, whose words of encouragement, insight, and love are stamped within and between the lines.

I am indebted to Eric Sellin for selecting many of these poems for publication in the *Literary Review*. My thanks go out, as well, to the MacDowell Colony, the Millay Colony for the Arts, and the 92nd Street Y/Unterberg Poetry Center.

I

Ahead, no singular, no grief.
Silicon retina, artificial cochlea, tongue:
we are learning how best to transcribe spirit
by tracking chemical release. To cobble
soul and sense together open here,
the nerve: insert. Localized
interior. My room looks west, and north;
late day's gray veneer aroused by breeze.
Months pass, moth-filled and uncontained,
since we slipped through ovals in San Marco's
dormer cells, looking down through glass to see
back toward black mountains' robed retreat,
blue fields, hands floating out of time.
It was neither mystical nor real, but it was both.
A thin lather of rain fell last night.
I woke at four again and listened to first birdcalls swerve
along the eaves. Voices scored for feeling
and depth: tassled, metallic rows of rants
unravel meridians. Immediate, unmediated world.
The talk here's about sacrifice—
Who would give up body first, who mind.
I try not to be seen or heard, though apparently
all we want is to be found.

*

Risen chambers along twigs of black gum,
butternut: buttercup playing Camaldoli's
forest floor. I held one to your chin, silence
stretching light's expanse between us. Measured
rhythms, equilibriums: that the shapes might
fit; mass to rhapsodic mass, vein to leaf, leaf
to branch; error to its thought; that in the symmetry
between hand and touch we might find not just relief.
I've lost track of how I've hurt you.
Out of stone huts hermits emerge

like mist's cargo, dissolve without blundering
into air. They'll come down the mountain
in old age. We watch from outside the gate—
Smoke curls skyward—

*

And darkness corked by light.
In this night scene the first bridge, built
out of the first man's mouth, makes the world make
sense. One theory says God fell in love and in letting go:
matter. Between death and dream breath's vanishing,
the broken parts, bring us back to each other—
erasures, secco-frescoed molecules—
malachite, ultramarine, lead tin yellow,
flaking with time, vine black triangles
where a branch once held the tree trembling in place.

A swarming, and then
The road bent into
Me. Foreground giving way
To brush, tree: spells
Clatter before they break.
Stone-encoded, chanted,
I was not clinging, not
Made of lack. Particulars
Rummaged (*soft, curable*).
But coming-to is distances
Unmoved through, the burned places
That return to haunt: posts and rails,
Swamps, studs — *weak, limber*
Bodies we arrive unrepaired
For. Hour of medicine, moon
Of sequestered spots, I'm
Someone else entirely.

FALSER CERTAINTY

Up all night at least for decades,
       hemlock trunks, wind's marathon-like
              dancers, veer reticently.
If they are not dead yet, then they are still alive,
       my story ends, whose characters
              became for each other: you the rosebush,
I the rose; you the church,
       I the chandelier;
              you the ring at the bottom of the pond.
Blue-chalk-ringed Norway
       Pine, Red Pine: whatever immortality's
              targeted you for is like the heart,
deceitful above all things. *Who can know it.*
       The sun's compact clicks shut; it won't come out
              again, not today, and leaves us
getting up for water, cautious, unreachable.
       I'm trying to learn the trees again, match
              line drawing to object, object to description:
unworldly thrill, world meeting
       words: white underlying needle-stripe confirms
              Northeast Balsam Fir, scars circular on the stalk—
naming's opening of landscape
       —false pleasure of falser certainty—
              as in a concept book: synthetic fur swatch
on the left page, and spelled out opposite
       in all caps, bold: *fur* and *soft*;
              no mistaking the sensation, no more
to want from or to give it—
       Watching you drive off—
              tree distorting into rose,
then chandelier, then church—
       No, in this story we can only be ourselves—
              if there's a message, it's not for us—
early moon staking, forsaking
       its lease on the forest now
              between us.

DE' FIORI

Relentless, stippled stars, fossil-
hitched, bone-housed: down
at Hotel Florida white shirts traverse
sleep's debris. Ten thousand lira extra buys
a breeze. Farther east, fireworks,
and a bridge of angels blurs one country
into the next. Earlier, crossing
toward historica's flowered square,
we mimed Tiber-frozen gestures
that defined us. Dazed, fast the city
rippled: exhausted distances receding
behind glass again. Rotating empty
space from sight to sight. Center-square's
where Bruno Giordano chose publicly to burn
rather than retrieve his worlds beyond
our world; unholy speeding universe;
and where uncored, wax-hollowed, doubly
removed, we slip away from touch.
The lost are like this. Let loose across
the jumbled sounds falling sideways makes:
how far's too far: how far beside oneself.

THE SUCCESSION OF PARTS

I. MEASURING SPACE

Our time 2 A.M., the engineer,
goggled, sealed in a chamber sealed from flames,
pilots like a racecar driver contracted
in his seat, his load gashed and bound
for a horizon this week's *Time*
debates the contents and the purpose of . . .
Unless we're all mistaken, which would alter
the age of rock and prove God has limits.
Endless possibilities to flounder in
may cause a cow, duped into the pleasures
of the afterworld, to resemble
an acrobat moored to an equally
obscene, obverse circus-type contraption,
scaling the tented hilt of the stage, spread-
eagled, finned against the floodlights. Encore!
Encore! the crowds beseech. A parched June night.
The vague arrival
of desperateness upon the wharf.
I need some help
to brave this fool's ship, it's off-course,
bungled in the unseen worlds that echo and dunk and rise
like marionettes dropped from the hieratic stars.

II. SPEED OF DESCENT

In *The Gospels*, villagers fall like stalks
and worship. Foraging for grounds to base
his beliefs upon, my friend reversed
a painting and found smatterings of ink
were really profiles of the five half-
faces outlined in suspension right-side up.
Fire converts matter from one form

to another, as paint does, and faith, and words.
I don't know anyone who's died in fire,
but when Linda's son rolled his kayak
underwater, his heart failed.
She said she woke up then from a dream.
      If there are spirits that pulse along the sill,
knock plants flat at midnight under chandeliers
that tingle and go dark, go to her.
Let her witness flame
promulgate into voice—
organism become element,
memory become more than the death
of love we're born to bear.
Let loose the oars, I said, and you did.
The waves hitched their skirts toward shore.
      Nine years I've counted you good as dead,
as if New Britain were an avatar of Heaven,
your jestered hair streaked gray or white.
Tonight I see my father in myself,
standing by the window looking blank
while small parades of neighbors shadow past.
Imagine Mary. Imagine driving to the funeral
after tea and crumpets, over saran-wrapped hills
where skiers synthesize the snow
into holy pods of light. Not Mary,
Linda. Tight-lipped in her vermilion dress,
scattering her spoors of ash. She gave him all.
      I've watched flesh burn in the city of golden
light and sung the praises of your deeper love
but I can't wheel my father from his side
of the blundering sea between us.
Loss is never random.
It's second nature, like bucking against
gravity in a dream of space just broken.

TAKE AIM

The cube's purpose on the shelf
is to be split open and reveal
a smaller version of itself—

to entice the hands to an end,
or a means to—
a bottom of things.

The closest one comes in this birch
wilderness to unity
is the car jostling

along the dirt road, charging the stoplight
just before it flashes to red,
the fogged peaks ululating in the view.

You believe, for an instant,
in your own exactness,
your own exultant, desultory,

neck-breaking speed. Oh the creature
comforts! Take pleasure
in your hearty composition,

the lovers who say
you should have been born
a fish, or a bird, the others who believe it.

BEECH TREE IN MARCH

Pale gold, acrylic gold,
       fledglings of wind-stream, slipstream,
late light's flexagon—where's the inroad?
       Frantic as netted fish—
       the movement's ocean-owned;
geometry takes the shape,
       conical, shirt-collar's inward curl against
sight; listening's the invitation. Listen. That upland-
       root-sucker's a festival, all ripple-
rattle, forest's confectioner, conductor of solar
       ellipses, earth's rumble seat.
I think it's giving lessons in gravity;
       Fagus grandifolia, single lamina bluntly
veined, fruit a prickly brown burr; wings coning
       along twigs; all morning I tried to see
it for what I wanted it to be:
       winged elm, a name that breathes
its sound; then tanbark, shingle oak; in truth,
saw-teeth and forest edge nearly pin
           it down as smooth sumac,
branches Elder-stout; in Europe's jardins
       it would be copper
           beech, weeping beech; here, behind my bark-
       built house, it's every inch American,
meaning in all likelihood, I'll wake to it, *cernere et videre*
           aliquide, tomorrow. For its open rounded crown
       bursting dead yellow on the scene
I'd profess a life of silence.
       "What they have a word for,
       they have a thing for," wrote Thoreau:
wilderness guide, spring's
       plagues, stacked
wheelbarrow, bud, open area,
           old field, roadside salute, cloudcover,
       post-strike, real time

beech, beech, beech,
       sturdy-toxic Ailanthus, shelter-shade
giver, Audubon's Tree-of-
       Heaven, identified by tolerance
for wet
       or dry or unspeakable conditions.

ENCHANTED

Speckle-breasted, rust-washed phrases rise
        and fall from log to wing-
                barred thicket. Last night,
July's shaved moon. *What are you afraid of?*
        peacocks cried, ruffling bougainvillea,
              palm. Once in a hammock,
by a palace, the day flayed open like a reed.
        It may be the story of our lives
             in which the hammock turns
to river, the palace to forest. No one
        gets forsaken. If I were a child
            enchanted by birds, would you know me
by my field marks, whorls? I'm heading
        North, cutting deals with time;
            come closer, swifts:
the moment before we turn
        to stone leaves us most deeply, most
            blazingly ajar—

BENARES

The first night.
Soldiers patrol the roofs above the swift,
punctured curves of alleyways,
orange strewn steps cascading down to the ghats.
An hour before prayer.
You lean over the rented canoe (*and the river wide running*),
offer petals in a lotus leaf for your father's mind,
corralled in the gloss of confusion
beyond method or embarrassment.
Downstream: the pyres (*do you wish to bring back the dead*),
ashes scattering over hills of stone and dung,
over ersatz gods and electric chambers
and plush nests of smoke and women multiplying on shore
(*and now the river cried out*) —
Let the offering slip away as quickly
(*for you will not be with me long*).
Let this image, exiled in a history not its own
(*and all the plain was parched and the shining water was striated*)
find its keeper among love's scatterings.

Sunstruck, terraced gables
      barnacled in marble heat
            we buy a right of passage through,
curves and countercurves, vista-spread:
      little Rome, Tivoli, bright Canopus,
            festooned and insistent. Be less
a dream. Be what you're supposed to be—
      scraped of color, phosphor-coated,
            spinning: in one battery of tests
I don't recover, suspended
            in continual relief, out of reach;
      land, love ravaged but real.
Olive and beech, frescoed thistle,
      slender, knobconed, triggered, peeled:
            all morning wending the autostrade's
erasure of fields, bowered distances—
      don't be dainty, I say, but silently,
come to me
      ceaselessly, with blows.

ON THE HOLY FRIAR CROSSING
A SUSPENSION BRIDGE TO PARADISE

The hollower the world
below, the more amplified

the music of his slip. One hundred fifty years
ago, at Monte Casale, he gave up speech,

shoes, waved off all his friends;
already he had fasted half

of every week, gone inanimate and
dumb and returned to matter whole.

Imagine swallowing your own teeth
and not feeling it. That's the real

world, not the one you're dreaming,
which has you running across a thorn-

sealed plain, tassle-briared, bleeding.
Your godparents, in flames, say *get up,*

for you have a greater journey.
Now the smoke-vague bridge,

unrailed, skate-narrow.
Step. For This Is. Halfway

he walked, and then grew
wings, and flapped, and dropped,

domed like a rib vault on its ridge.
Three times he tried, and failed,

and then he flew.

*

Unless Paradise comes at the beginning
of the story, in which case

he should have remained a robber,
looting alms instead of begging

them. But this is not a story—
as *ice frond* isn't, or *fishgut*,

or the paleography of jagged stones
scrawled across the field, familiar

of bare feet, of frost's call—
monovalent forever

and forever assembling itself
beneath the shrouded zodiac.

This is only the unsequenced clatter
of crossing—

only the unhoused hours you keep
falling through, rapture

of the body receding,
a single vanishing point.

CONVERSION

A horse white among the drizzling trees.
　　　　The field made for calling
names. *Bernardo*. Because sound, unanswered,
　　　　receives him. No night for. No night of.
Inkblot, blanket—Earth is deeper
　　　　than it is complete. And walking home,
for the last time: four cypresses high
　　　　along a plane; rain's portioned sky
recovering, from his memory, the drunken
　　　　fall of silk. Its surface breathes
until the night becomes its palimpsest—
　　　　obverse, reverse. The world seems
soft then. Back in the old streets (shuttered,
　　　　ringing) stones will be laid on
stones, him naked in the square.
　　　　Faces at their windows—
But here the carnival branches, concealed,
　　　　unaccountable, form a kind of mirror
for his vanishing. His lopsided footsteps
　　　　don't seem like a fiction,
the phrases to describe them.
　　　　I am no longer your . . . he practices.
Sed sine te non valeo.
　　　　Air has another side, like water.

No one really waits forever.
Father, shrunken in the noon-sleep he's aged
into, his leg's sensation lost,
looted of his angered self, panics.
Undisguise your voice of shady reassurances,
and sit with him. Come here. Teach me
to sit with my father. Give this crumb

of unattainable delight. I'll bring
him orphaned shells from the porch
and what he hears inside them will be the hush
and billow of the waves. I'll believe him.
No one will keen: at least he didn't suffer,
at least he held onto his memory,
at least he had his sight. Is love most required

when it's most unsafe? St. Francis wanted God's
so terribly he vowed to stand outside
a shelter, cudgeled, profaned through snow
and rain and say, This is perfect joy.
Love, all suffering and willingness.
Beneath the insatiate elms he'd wait,
muddy, barefoot in his shepherd's cloak,

the doorkeeper staring, slurring *rascal*,
thief through the pleated air, refusing him
both entrance and food. Reading, we know
how at the end of the little flowers,
how soon with eyes diseased he'd lie on bare
ground like some early Lear and say take off
my garments, unbutton me here . . .

I meant to speak better. I meant to ask
my father one essential thing, just once
to tell him he's essential, not to still

act the keeper, guarding fast the door,
saying nothing I mean, gawking from my
porthole, copping a feel of the impending
storm, dawdling, dawdling, dumb and trusting
that, the hour close at hand, I'd let him in.

DIRECTIONS

Rehearse the scene where perspective
is weeded out—spend your whole life
in the forest hemmed in by leaves
and whispers, and the plain, when you reach
it or are forced to its edge,
is bound to kill something in you.
Who can convince the eye
that the tree (that one, there—
a slippery elm) never seen from afar,
didn't just now float in, swallow-small?
Distance is relative, and shameful:
not a day ends without our figures
conjoined in it, shadows or shades,
though ten years have passed.
There are countless ways to hate oneself.
Keep staring: the tree doesn't grow
any taller, but you live with it.
You stop faltering.
Rub lightly and the landscape,
in slight relief, lies down in you.

PIAN DELL'ARCA

You walk into the field hiding
        your hands in your sleeves. You imagine,
as you turn toward the elms, a god—
        arms outspread above the fish-scaled leaves,
the tipped scale of birds pressing down—
        watching you, whispering your name.
At the bleached grass you begin counting your steps.
        Your father—how many unsaid words behind?—
from a dream beckons for you,
        and soon the desire to hear him speak,
to lie down in his hands,
        reels you forward through the hours.
What's left is a house empty on the hill.
        The field is an ending, by accident
or solitude, you have broken into.
        You will learn its language.
You will bend toward its refracted messages,
        a begging son, unused to it.
The pieces of you moving so fast
        they seem to merge.

COMING OF AGE

In one initiation ritual in New Guinea, a young woman, dressed as a deity, was
brought to lie down beneath a great, makeshift roof; several young boys were led to
her, one after another, for their first sexual experience. "When the last boy was
with her, in full embrace, the supports were withdrawn, the logs dropped, and the
couple were killed . . ." —Joseph Campbell, Sacrifice and Bliss

I. RITUAL

The boy takes his turn inside the hut upheld by pillars *today shalt thou be*
with me in paradise and lies atop the girl face up in the center *gather*
the fragments that remain stolen paroxysms of desire *that nothing be lost*
between the props and pillars yielding the children's job here is to stay afloat
intractable for even Jesus went singing to the sacrifice *then shall they begin*
to say to the mountains: Fall on us; and to the hills, cover us
his father built this hut for them they are the garden of delights the first
and the last do not look up keep moving the pillars yielding *that nothing*
be lost crushed their flesh becomes word again each lovesick breath
unseparating the world *I am the voice of one crying in the wilderness*
wild multitude arising *that they may also be one in us* take, eat
for this is the kingdom domed above them the end of their desires yielding
wherefore unto this day the things seen are the things that *are.*
This end is called, *The kingdom come.*

We lie between two mountains—
brothers, T. told us, that legend says
had fought so viciously over Mt. St. Helens
the Great One shoved a gorge between them.
A warbler on the new plum.
You say it could be an oriole or a goldfinch,
but I remember the poem for you anyway:
we hardened ourselves to live by.
Then a mole rippling the ground beneath us.
We drove 3000 miles with the windows shut.
Constructed our family trees, reconstructed,
somewhere between the Badlands and the Black Hills, your father,
disappearing now in a basement behind blinded doors.
Promise you won't let me suffer. Like that man.
The birds, meantime, gather on the wire,
twenty of them jerking their tight tufted heads side to side.
The eyes skinned of memory, does every second strike fully, as it happens?
How I wanted, west on 90, the sky spoonfeeding the Bozeman peaks,
to look at you long enough that whatever veil
stops the moment from feeling real
suddenly lifts, the way the backwater,
too cold to stick a toe in, shuns us.
Your father ran seven years barefoot through the forest.
Chased, barefoot through the forest;
stuffed to hide inside a haystack
his mind all gone he still bears the pitchfork marks.
I'll never meet him.
I'll never say, to you, I want to make it whole
to the afterlife, with you
I want to get there whole.

II

WAVE

Tell the truth: no key appeared in your mouth,
no sound like *mum*, which wouldn't help anyway.
Give me a word to get through the night.
Something spontaneous, fluid:
see the hand's unintended imprint on the shore,

fireworks dissolving into the black sky—

      Try now. *Ripple*. Yes.
Put the two of us in a boat on the gray river;
keep rowing in a circle while on the hazy banks
clumps of grass swarm and echo the rhythm of words
we had once spoken: *after this, mistake me for someone else*.
Sleep no more. Wave. Wave. That's love enough.

TRACE OF ONE

Where they walk he tells her the secrets of trees:
orange inside Black Oak bark,
how Aspen grows on burnt-over

land. Her steps form the grammar
of her silence. Something

between distance and fear,
        listening to herself listening.

Boxwood, excelsior. Pulp.

(In winter she used to follow him
        across the brittle tracks, the ice.

Beneath them the water toughened.)

Ahead of them now, the rustling sun.
She wants his voice to be for her
        a room without a pattern, without a history.

        He seeks a language between field

and forest. He seeks an hour
when memory, broken, turns transparent
        (*these words will also be broken*).

Then the landscape again,
        their solitudes replaced by the first light.
        A spot where disappearing begins.

HOW DID YOU COME TO KNOW

Particles deposit close to shore:
os and isthmus, heart bulge, leg bud,
a rudimentary eye. The view is straight
inside. Out of your belly flow rivers slaked
on erasure. Look: past visible light, past
microwave and infrared, in magnetics' field
quadrille of photons, the axis flaps and folds.
Slowly now. Put on these socks. They're made
of snow and leaf scar. Take with you
this cup. Fill it with the wings
of sphenoids. What you would do, do quickly:
unscore Paradise from its geography.
This gown is paper and will burn.
Of blind, of halt, of withered —Patience.
The soul functions without word or sign.
See this opening? Enter and be shattered.

REASONS FOR EVERYTHING

For a while there was still more to build on:
quarter-light's periphery outlining
ampulla and fimbria, primary follicle—
entrenched meander of the child
we had come to see better.
For faith we might have stopped
before the laboratory door, turned out
toward sun-encrusted corners,
giving up our urge to TV-view
the strangeness of her heart.
We thought we'd hear the beat.
The day hadn't even been called a day—
Hope something's there, I joked—
No reply—but later, *the body's body
can die and give no outward sign.*

Come, it's not yet dark. Settle bills—
my disposable slippers disposed, thank you,
thank you, I blamed them all for the part of me
that wanted out—and left.
If there are reasons for everything,
failure's favorite line, let reason let it go—
I'll hang on a little for time's barehanded
sake, for the part that ended
with her ending, and say what?
Something in me always chooses
to tear silently away? All of it:
don't be afraid, I mean for myself.
Once across a paper mat we scratched
her name out from ancient sounds,
then fearing hexes, hid it even from ourselves.
Tonight's a moon-festooned spectacle, gregarious,
celestial in coats of snow. From cracked cavities
it slips unbroken. While stars like batter pour.

OF FORCE AND DISTANCE

They lost and in their losing gained.
One way to live forever, they remarked,
was to forever age. It's energy runs us amuck:
had none of them had any, a hell to make
a mind of might not rage; imagine marshland
for the will, no flood of flame to pissquick through;
and for shame, a hurling into boundless

praise: this loss of field, this fate
you've deep-sixed, stupefied and transfixed
from, wouldn't find you pulling out the block
and tackle from your throat, wouldn't rally
your fallen parts, or leave you flat on your back,
wanting to make good the stay.

WHERE TO END

At the sill, where the absence of light
meets the absence of sound.
Where hung blankets keep out the cold,
where the edge of glass becomes the edge

of the barred sky and winter, balancing
its green shade over valed floodplains,
in wrappings keeps the things we fear.
Awake side by side, there is nothing

to let us go. Come back across the dirt-
cankered road, to the first house. Tell me
how long I've arranged, rearranged this story,
this longing where no details remain.

PORT DE GRAVE

I

Bough-restricted boundary,
wind-inflated brambles and rife-in-the-mouth forest—
What is deeply lost
proclaims itself, for the fifth time this morning, gone.
Red sidereal leaves, a turning back
to autumn's trampled coruscant.
I'll give up building, said Vokey,
when I'm not able to get in the woods —
and that'll be soon probably —
when I can't even get in the woods to get it —
meaning the spruce or juniper
he'd, looking up from below, see
as stern and sternpost, apron, knee, breasthook.

—Untempered sunset, August night, clothespin-hung.
Caplin, *Mallotus villosus*, roll by thousands in;
darting, black, puncture-twitch; they proscenium-carve
the shallow of the bay, draw from dusk an audience;
cod's moratorium masses fishermen, boot-deep, instead
of sea-, to lower rust-hewn pails into their congregations—
all of us, tacked up moon, imagining—

II

Sharp, ariatic, winded-wince—
breath's recall, half habit, half
affect with which our neighbor punctuates
each phrase. What do the Jews believe,
exactly——? Words' aftermath.
Sudden ambassadors of what we don't know
but as suddenly should: color of bulrush, what plagues,
Abrahams' *put your hand beneath my thigh and promise,*

the cave at the end of the field.
Churches measure miles here,
a Pentecostal, penta-coastal town,
Catholic graveyards in decay, flattened
by sea and seasons' cruelty.
Bill's family never left this road,
its coves, Come by Chance, Little Hearts,
Blow Me Down. We watch his mother,
varicose-veined, wrestler-legged,
straddle a torn foam plastic chair,
shell Sunday's peas. Forty years ago
her husband, father of three,
night-walking the steep cliff's edge to our left,
slipped and drowned. He knew the curves well;
there's nothing to ask, or tell.

III

And that'll be soon probably . . .
too soon, probably.
Eternity, angels are the present business,
not our strong suit, who've just weeks ago
reached the age, talking at candled dinners
under signs that bless this home,
of fathers dying. I call mine, too often,
pushing back the stop; nothing to say,
I feign interest in fish, still not the daughter
I telephone to be. Tallis-shrouded, the sea
davens, sidling in its robes.
We all have ways of keeping the dead safe;
your father's safer dead, unwrapped
from drool-stained sheets.
What will you be now?
Blackened mirrors mean stand back, look elsewhere.
The dissolving waves themselves an ending.
Every word itself an ending, breath's currency.

DEPARTURE

after Max Beckmann

I am standing neck-deep in a barrel of water.
I am calling out the name of my street.
And through the black ribbon around my eyes:
corundum, drumfish, corvina, coshboy.

       Wherever I go, I am always the one to play the Blind Man.

My head tilted back, my hands in the air,
a glass-blown wave.

Outside bombs were exploding.
I walked to her house across fields of dry grass,
I knocked on the door with the flat of my hand, once, twice.
Her with a bottle of water and a basin for my soiled hands.
Her pouring water on my hands. I was old then.
I told her about a garden, about a barren tree upheld by stones,
about crows pinned to the branches. She stood all night
by the window. The ground rocked on its iron horse.
I said, *Could you love me?*
The color of the sky was the color of shrapnel.
The trains looked made of lead.
Alone on a red stool I heard people passing behind the church,
heard the roofs falling from buildings
and soldiers rubbing their knees.
Every word is the sacrifice of another word, another sound.
I whisper our names into a candle.
Light blows through the curtains. I mean to lie down
but the song of the bells curdles in the air
and my hands are full of feathers.
We'll build ourselves in ivory, we'll build ourselves
in pauses, we'll build ourselves in clutter.

WHAT BROUGHT THEM THERE

Two children escape the bombed city
through alleys, whispering *Elijah*. They have heard

that to get closer to God you must run
with bandages on your eyes. Their father hangs

from a windmill; he was the man who carried

stones from the pasture. Which way does one turn
to not betray oneself? The pasture was prepared

for sacrifice. History is the windmill
churning. Is the remaining tree. The children run

until the motion of their legs defines

the shape of the hours, until their running
reifies the city, until

we cannot picture ourselves, the light, the whole

breathing landscape not in the act of escape.

THE AFTERMATH

My child jumped from a tree onto my back. Night dropped
    its green awning.

And walking away from the woods we saw roads opening out into roads.
We saw birds lifting from steam, and we did not look away
from the bricks breaking in pieces where houses should have been.
We did not look away when the trucks came, carrying ash.

We climbed up a ladder, slipped inside the ruin.
And the window was an eyelid, sifting air.

I imagined I was someone else, finding us.

I heard a woman call *Gabriel, Gabriel*.
Up ahead, pages turned. A voice said, *This is the left side of God*.
Then the chimneys caving in, and the stars piercing the inside darkness.

My child and I walk across shingles. I whisper, *The sea is not far*.

And then, for the first time, I sleep with my arms tight around him.
I stare at his back until I see double.

No, I sit on a metal chair. He stands

with his hands on my shoulders.
I say, *How long have you stood here with your hands on my shoulders?*

RESUSCITATION

My father picks up the phone to hear the sound of fire.
I walk from room to room looking inside books.
Planes hum along the shaft of sky; our voices
part from our words. There is nowhere left to hide.

My father stands by an open door.
His eyes form screens through which birds fly.
He shapes a fortress with his thumbs,
whispering, *Saint Aloysius, Saint Aloysius*.

The moon uncovers the dark like a grand auctioneer.

These are the days of sleeping, of watching for friends,
of imagining rising above the bed, small, winged, turning.
Standing before my father as if he were the memory of my father.
My father asking, *Is it you?*

Nothing can hear us, I say.

Saint Aloysius has one hand in the air, beckoning down comrades.

This, the second ending, the one we keep living through.

RECITATIVE

When you're the last one left and out
of fountained air a voice speaks, by God
it is no miracle. *Sursum corda*:
you're not the chosen. For failing
to distinguish the hoary redpoll
from the kinglet, arrowhead from spear—
wake up when kissed, wash thoroughly your feet
or carry music in your ear; for never having walked
through darkness upright or sung amongst the trees,
for taking no one with you and for spitting
the poison from your cup; for making not one brick
from straw, and for gathering not the straw;
for stealing wishbones; for hoarding clavicles;
for the dead fish; and for the dead child,
sursum corda, sursum corda, you're not the one.

THE DRY SPELL

We weren't allowed anything sharp so we rocked back and forth
   in the garden.
The guards held flashlights over our bodies. I returned only for you
with my volunteer pass and my open bag, each Friday at twelve.
There was a dry spell that summer which climbed up the hardback fence
between Northampton State and the town. We took it in like succulents,
hovering over the tulips with our picks, with our troublesome spines.
In early June God shouted up through your sheets that I was your wife.
You told me our lost ones swell out of ourselves during the dry seasons.
I looked after you like all my losses,
I called you by names that had been taken from me.
I lay next to you still as a root with our heads in the tulips.
Most of all I loved how you couldn't leave,
I loved you locked up with a cigarette on the hour,
   waiting and incurable;
I saw myself come unconstrained in you the way soil gives under water.
Forgive me, Michael; It was all an experiment.
September came and I named you Timothy to protect you.
I left you walking the same hundred yards all night
out to where the buildings have atrophied
with two thousand spirits still looking for something sharp inside.

AFTER BEING CALLED NAÏVE, I CONSULT
THE SINGLE SOURCE FOR PEOPLE
WHO NEED TO BE RIGHT

Now that I am finally, affirmatively *there*

let me be beside myself a little;
let the snowman in mystery sink,
the haystack fill with languor, straw's reams

fill with languor, the land itself,
bare rooms partaking of archaic cold:
this morning I learned to walk

through overlaps of risen snow; I think I was learning to walk;
Oh diphthong of *joy*, single outright sound
contribution of Norman French,

oh pater, pater, pater, birchen bark
and squash. *Language is fossil poetry*,
said Emerson, like soft rock quashed

in harder rock, eroding to form rapids.
The wind in mismatched blasts unfurls
high firs, majestic heads nodding assent:

langue d'oc, langue d'oil, in seconds reaching
the end of earth, wings beating without end
into the effortless sky unbroken;

you, who watched the lightning sing,
would that you not miss the darkness in your mouth.
Wild and inscrutable: don't disappear.

EXAMPLES OF USE

Golden light churning the river
during the season of street-diggers.
The room in which I held an iron
for the first time.
Wave. Wave to it—the heat,
the golden, golden hush. Hush now.
One must bend over the board:
jostle the steam from its holes

as breathing
empties the breather out.
Straighten up and the world
spits back its images:
my name splintering on and off
against the digging. My keeper, my keeper,
you're always in the background.
Didn't you swear I'd turn out better?
This is the 10th floor.
It's dark. The residents are listening.

WHAT YOU CAN EXPECT THIS MONTH

Quasi-twitch beneath the breastplate,
gourd-roll hatched inside, while, out,
pigeons scrap and prong along the fault
adjoining roofs. I want a rope to Malta.
I want to see in Malta horsehair clouds
and Jane's drowned syllables spread
through blue, gluey light. See, doctor,
not everyday's as gutted as the last.
Just now rubbernecking on the verandah
seemed a thrill and I remembered Jane
chopping herring on her stepstool.
Bent and lurching, she'd rifle through
her jewel box, going blind.
We waited with our little mouths
fishhook-slit for the tiniest of tastes,
make-believing none of us
could see. Oh, clamor of signs,
don't hesitate. Cane it. Hobble toward.

COMING UP VIOLETS

To escape danger unscathed, better off
even, is to come up smelling of violets.
But you're not a remarkably lucky
person. Stare blindly at the ocean

like you're one with its collapsings and, while
passersby admire your steadfastness
in the face of wind and tide, the starving
feeling in your heart kicks in. Sailing torn

sheets through fog invisible to others,
signaling distress to the shorehouse,
a store-bought whale keening for the kill,
you'd always founder back to bed

alive, game over, wounded but alive.
I like thinking that in hurricanes or war
my hundred votives would last the darkness,
my partridgeberry jam, my dimes, my books,

I take precautions, take two kinds of pills
so as to shake less in my sleep, so as not
to anchor down in an amputated ward
putting on my face for visitors—

—Mrs. Almer, Sue—*Let's Make a Deal* blared
through the TV room; we joked down her vision
of the blessed ghosts crooning inside vents,
hoisting their cargo skyward after her sure

collision—*next week*, she said, *tomorrow.*
I loved her son and her and lost

them both. March. I'm ten months past my mother's
age when, half-dressed, curled on the kitchen floor,
she too promised not to see the light of day
again, suddenly unsuburban, just as suddenly

revived by an electric prong, the delicate twig
of her body shocked upward before
struck dumb again with sadness.
Once, driving her green Beetle in a storm

across Fish's Eddy bridge, she wrested
an Eskimo girl who rolled down snow-thick hills,
puffing bigger as she dashed until,
unrecognizable, abundant,

bundled in her vessel, she clocked back home
intact. At least that's how I remember
that heavy weather now, though medics
never shocked her out of it, she simply

didn't disappear. I stopped expecting her
to disappear. Imagine the girl
bursting from her ball, only it's not snow,
it's fire, and the live coal bridled to her

doesn't hurt, it's the fear we're born with.

THE MOON SMILED CHEEKILY

Wave-cradled corded bundles,
gulls timer-posed on stumps of wood.
I may be the type to leave and not
return, or one who never leaves,
but should. The steps end here in mid-
air. Doctor, however rigged to things
I'm told I am, however weedy
and continuous, the train blows
water fern soft; empty, browsing,
river wind; and I'm still behind
the window breaking hours into color,
color into synapse. Explain again—

a place to lodge my entering
all wrong. It's the way you say *approach*
I can't resist. Let's try a succulent, tertiary
one. The boats stretch longer upriver,
or the river's longer, or there's more space
for image, end. Lend me a hand. The flower
of milk. *I don't have a particular face when I cry,*
a bulky father says ahead, screwing his into one.

HOME

A bit lickerish and dissolute,
testing your own get-up-and-go,
you call stars cankers on the sky.
Quel bravado! Clever monkey.
The parts of you in love with you
stand agog. Pull your curtain string,
seek comfort in your balderdash—

the mind God gave you, that little piece
of purgatory, never satisfying.
You might escape into the dreaming hours,
but the night wasn't, you know, made for you.
Find in yourself that substance you crave
for sleep, mulch-thick, peat.

Oh sweet. How girlish your behavior.
You weren't put on this earth to fester.
When your parents fall to their knees
on the corded rug, a hall away, be stout
in your gaze. Be their lovely again.
You, for whom love is rage,

unguard your door, come through.
Father whispers, "little one."
You dangle on a stick—go thither, queen bee,
go nigh. Help them up.
Here liquid takes the shape of its container.
The instructions are almost over.
You're almost lost without them.

LAWS OF MOTION

I lie on the red couch with my mother.
Lucy is getting drunk, slurring her words.
Another swig, and then the commercial

break. *I should have been on stage*,
exclaims my mother, donning her tophat.
Once in love with Amy, always in love

with Amy. My father wakes
out of his sleeping role, says my name,
the raw material from which someone

sturdy could be made,
someone who could leave
a mark. Clap and clap. The laughing

stock. Gasp and laugh.
We who would always
be members of each other's

audience, didn't know.
Who's the mother of the nine muses?
Memory. A brief madness.

IN AN EXCESSIVE CORRIDOR

The story is always one of axing
your way out only to end
more deeply interiored—
not river anymore, but sea, ghostly;
neither does it try to retain a shape,
being shape itself, being form,
and motion after which we
pattern our steps. Deflecting
and deflecting: look, turtles jitter
in my palm, fragile pilgrims
of undersand's underbelly,
of sawgrass and sediment, longshore's drift.
We know the rules: dig them up, just born,
hustle them to shore, to make the right
turn, toward sea's glare instead of beach-
front pools, halogen-tempting.
At least one's got a shot at a deeper end—
polar bottom, Ekman spiral, marine's eden.
What month again—on that rock to our right, awash
in afterwash, you wiped a seat, married me.
It was a good plan. Now the second upsurge
shadow-skids behind: scurrilous,
crooning heads resist withdrawal,
confused. We are not quick enough.
Contingencies escape us,
both chosen against and missed.
There's a cruelty to perspective.
In many worlds they carry the world.
In many worlds the story begins
right now, for those who rush for the light,
now water, now sky, now electric.

The title "Tebaide" is taken from a series of paintings ("Scenes from a Monastic Life") by Paolo Uccello and refers to an ideal place where monks live in silence and serene isolation.

Line four (*If they are not dead yet, then they are still alive*) of "Falser Certainty" is borrowed from the last line of "Fundevogel" by the Brothers Grimm (Viking Press, 1973).

The title "de' Fiori" refers to Rome's Campo de' Fiori, or Square of Flowers. *The lost are like this* is from Gerard Manley Hopkins's "I wake and feel."

Cernere et videre aliquide in "Beech Tree in March" means *to see clearly, distinctly*. A flexagon is a mathematical paper-folding game that creates an illusion of transformed images when the paper is bent.

The italicized lines in "Benares" are slightly altered phrases from Homer's *The Iliad* (trans. Richard Lattimore, University of Chicago Press, 1951) and the Bible, King James Version.

The title "A Light Arch of Cloud, Ten Fingers Wide" is borrowed from an ancient mariner's proverb.

Lines 14–15 (*get up/for you have a greater journey*) of "On the Holy Friar Crossing a Suspension Bridge to Paradise" is from W. Heywood's translation of *The Little Flowers of St. Francis of Assisi* (Vintage, 1998).

Sed sine te non valeo in "Conversion" is by Catullus and means *without you, I'm nothing*.

Pian dell'Arca is the plain where St. Francis preached to the birds.

Part I of "Coming of Age" includes phrases from the Bible, King James Version. They appear in italics. In Part II of the poem, the phrase *we hardened ourselves to live by* is from "Meditation Celestial and Terrestrial" by Wallace Stevens.

Port de Grave is a town in Newfoundland. Henry Vokey, a master boatbuilder from the province's Trinity Bay, named his vessels after his daughters.

Sursum corda in "Recitative" means *lift up your hearts.*

1987

Elton Glaser, *Tropical Depressions*

Michael Pettit, *Cardinal Points*

1988

Bill Knott, *Outremer*

Mary Ruefle, *The Adamant*

1989

Conrad Hilberry, *Sorting the Smoke*

Terese Svoboda, *Laughing Africa*

1990

Philip Dacey, *Night Shift at the Crucifix Factory*

Lynda Hull, *Star Ledger*

1991

Greg Pape, *Sunflower Facing the Sun*

Walter Pavlich, *Running near the End of the World*

1992

Lola Haskins, *Hunger*

Katherine Soniat, *A Shared Life*

1993

Tom Andrews, *The Hemophiliac's Motorcycle*

Michael Heffernan, *Love's Answer*

John Wood, *In Primary Light*

1994

James McKean, *Tree of Heaven*

Bin Ramke, *Massacre of the Innocents*

Ed Roberson, *Voices Cast Out to Talk Us In*

1995

Ralph Burns, *Swamp Candles*

Maureen Seaton, *Furious Cooking*

1996

Pamela Alexander, *Inland*

Gary Gildner, *The Bunker in the Parsley Fields*

John Wood, *The Gates of the Elect Kingdom*

1997

Brendan Galvin, *Hotel Malabar*

Leslie Ullman, *Slow Work through Sand*

1998

Kathleen Peirce, *The Oval Hour*

Bin Ramke, *Wake*

Cole Swensen, *Try*

1999

Larissa Szporluk, *Isolato*

Liz Waldner, *A Point Is That Which Has No Part*

2000

Mary Leader, *The Penultimate Suitor*

2001

Joanna Goodman, *Trace of One*

Karen Volkman, *Spar*